MATH ACADEMY

GROUPS
IN THE
GARDEN

By Kirsty Holmes

CRABTREE
PUBLISHING COMPANY
WWW.CRABTREEBOOKS.COM

CRABTREE
PUBLISHING COMPANY
WWW.CRABTREEBOOKS.COM

Author:
  Kirsty Holmes
Editorial director:
  Kathy Middleton
Editors:
  William Anthony, Janine Deschenes
Proofreader:
  Crystal Sikkens
Graphic design:
  Ian McMullen
Prepress technician:
  Katherine Berti
Print coordinator:
  Katherine Berti

All images are courtesy of Shutterstock.com, unless otherwise specified. With thanks to Getty Images, Thinkstock Photo, and iStockphoto.

Front Cover: Potapov Alexander, Werner Muenzker, Valentina Razumova, Iryna B, Kenishirotie, primiaou, Ola_view

Interior: Background – ngaga. Characters: Maya: Rajesh Narayanan. Zoe: Dave Pot. Robert: Shift Drive. Abdul: Ahmad Ihsan. Professor Tengent: Roman Samborskyi. Cy-Bud: AlesiaKan. 6 – napas chalermchai, oksana2010. 8 – Valentyn Volkov. 10 – Antonova Ganna. 11 – Florin Burlan, carroteater, Diana Taliun. 14 – Madlen timquo. 16 – bergamont, Kovaleva_Kat. 18 – Elena Zajchikova. 19 – Hurst Photo. 21 – margouillat photo. 22 – bergamont. 23 – AlenKadr, Robyn Mackenzie, Lotus Images

All facts, statistics, web addresses, and URLs in this book were verified as valid and accurate at time of writing. No responsibility for any changes to external websites or references can be accepted by either the author or publisher.

Library and Archives Canada Cataloguing in Publication

Title: Groups in the garden / by Kirsty Holmes.
Names: Holmes, Kirsty, author.
Description: Series statement: Math academy | Includes index.
Identifiers: Canadiana (print) 2020039410X |
  Canadiana (ebook) 20200394169 |
  ISBN 9781427130105 (hardcover) |
  ISBN 9781427130143 (softcover) |
  ISBN 9781427130181 (HTML)
Subjects: LCSH: Counting—Juvenile literature. | LCSH: Addition—
  Juvenile literature. | LCSH: Set theory—Juvenile literature.
Classification: LCC QA113 .H65 2021 | DDC j513.2/11—dc23

Library of Congress Cataloging-in-Publication Data

Available at the Library of Congress

Crabtree Publishing Company

www.crabtreebooks.com   1–800–387–7650
Published by Crabtree Publishing Company in 2021
© 2020 BookLife Publishing Ltd.

Printed in the U.S.A./022021/CG20201123

Published in Canada
Crabtree Publishing
616 Welland Ave.
St. Catharines, Ontario
L2M 5V6

Published in the United States
Crabtree Publishing
347 Fifth Ave
Suite 1402-145
New York, NY 10016

CONTENTS

Words that are bold, like **this**, can be found in the glossary on page 24.

Another day at Math Academy has begun. Time to take attendance! Meet some students in class 301.

Maya
Favorite subject:
Place value

Zoë
Favorite subject:
Counting in groups

Professor Tangent

Ali
Favorite subject:
Addition

Robert
Favorite subject:
Subtraction

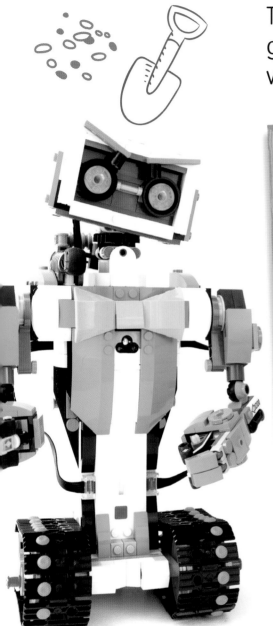

Today's lesson is all about **counting** in groups and **skip counting**. The students will learn answers to these questions.

- What is skip counting?

- What are the different ways we can count groups?

- How can a hundreds chart help us skip count?

Math Academy is a school especially for kids who love math and solving problems.

Do I hear the bell?

Cy-Bud

Favorite subject: Facts and figures

This morning, the students in class 301 are working outside in the Math Academy garden. It is a sunny day and the fruits and vegetables in the garden are growing bigger.

I am so proud of my students. The garden helps them make healthy food choices and learn how plants grow.

☐ Pumpkins

☐ Corn

☐ Cucumbers

☐ Strawberries

☐ Blueberries

Today, the class will count how many fruits and vegetables have grown from the **seeds** they planted back in the spring. It is Ali's job to write the **total** numbers down.

LUNCHTIME

Ali takes the list around the garden while the other children work on counting the fruits and vegetables. Robert is counting the blueberries, but he seems to have a problem.

Zoë can see that counting the blueberries one at a time will take a long time. There are too many of them. Robert needs a faster way to count the large number of blueberries.

You could count in groups, Robert. That way, you can count the blueberries much more quickly.

The other students gather around Zoë. Everyone wants to know how to count faster! Zoë explains counting one-by-one makes sense when there are only a few items to count. She points to the pumpkins. There are just five pumpkins growing on the vine.

It doesn't take long to count to 5!

5 Pumpkins

When there are a lot of items to count, it is quicker to count in groups. It is easiest to count groups that have the same number of items. This is called skip counting.

Groups of 1

Skip counting means we skip some numbers when we count. We can skip count by any number: twos, fours, one hundreds, and more.

Groups of 4

Groups of 2 (pairs)

Groups of 100

A hundreds chart can help make skip counting easier. It has rows of numbers from one to 100.

The hundreds chart helps me see which numbers come next when I skip count.

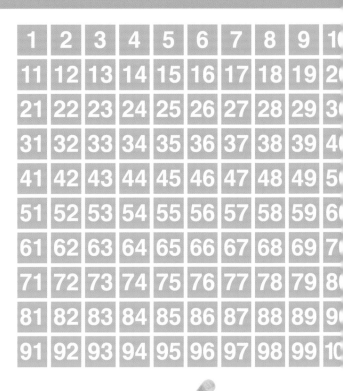

1	2	3	4	5	6	7	8	9	10
11	12	13	14	15	16	17	18	19	20
21	22	23	24	25	26	27	28	29	30
31	32	33	34	35	36	37	38	39	40
41	42	43	44	45	46	47	48	49	50
51	52	53	54	55	56	57	58	59	60
61	62	63	64	65	66	67	68	69	70
71	72	73	74	75	76	77	78	79	80
81	82	83	84	85	86	87	88	89	90
91	92	93	94	95	96	97	98	99	100

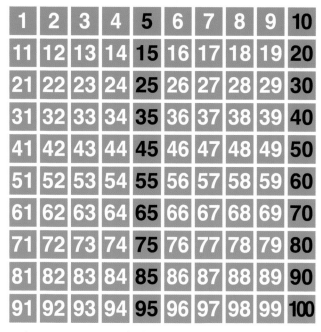

1	2	3	4	5	6	7	8	9	10
11	12	13	14	15	16	17	18	19	20
21	22	23	24	25	26	27	28	29	30
31	32	33	34	35	36	37	38	39	40
41	42	43	44	45	46	47	48	49	50
51	52	53	54	55	56	57	58	59	60
61	62	63	64	65	66	67	68	69	70
71	72	73	74	75	76	77	78	79	80
81	82	83	84	85	86	87	88	89	90
91	92	93	94	95	96	97	98	99	100

When we count by twos, or in groups of two, we count every second number.

1	2	3	4	5	6	7	8	9	10
11	12	13	14	15	16	17	18	19	20
21	22	23	24	25	26	27	28	29	30
31	32	33	34	35	36	37	38	39	40
41	42	43	44	45	46	47	48	49	50
51	52	53	54	55	56	57	58	59	60
61	62	63	64	65	66	67	68	69	70
71	72	73	74	75	76	77	78	79	80
81	82	83	84	85	86	87	88	89	90
91	92	93	94	95	96	97	98	99	100

When we count by fives, or in groups of five, we count every fifth number.

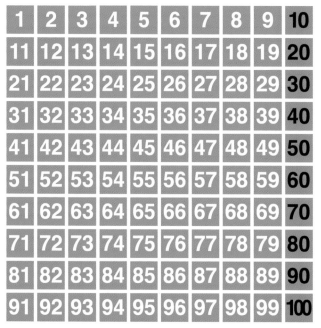

1	2	3	4	5	6	7	8	9	10
11	12	13	14	15	16	17	18	19	20
21	22	23	24	25	26	27	28	29	30
31	32	33	34	35	36	37	38	39	40
41	42	43	44	45	46	47	48	49	50
51	52	53	54	55	56	57	58	59	60
61	62	63	64	65	66	67	68	69	70
71	72	73	74	75	76	77	78	79	80
81	82	83	84	85	86	87	88	89	90
91	92	93	94	95	96	97	98	99	100

When we count by tens, or in groups of ten, we count every tenth number.

There are six corn **stalks** in the Math Academy garden. Each stalk has two **cobs** of corn growing on it. The students can skip count the cobs of corn by twos.

The cobs of corn are already in groups of two! This makes it easier to skip count by twos.

The students use the hundreds chart to help them count the corn. They start at 2 and count every second number. They stop when they have counted all six plants.

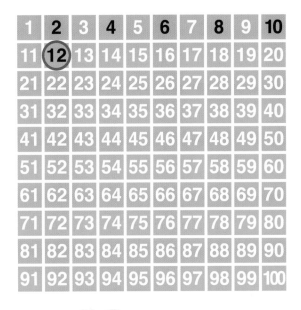

1	2	3	4	5	6	7	8	9	10
11	12	13	14	15	16	17	18	19	20
21	22	23	24	25	26	27	28	29	30
31	32	33	34	35	36	37	38	39	40
41	42	43	44	45	46	47	48	49	50
51	52	53	54	55	56	57	58	59	60
61	62	63	64	65	66	67	68	69	70
71	72	73	74	75	76	77	78	79	80
81	82	83	84	85	86	87	88	89	90
91	92	93	94	95	96	97	98	99	100

There are 12 cobs of corn in total.

12 Corn

There are ten cucumber plants in the garden. Each cucumber plant has five cucumbers growing on it. The students can skip count the cucumbers by fives.

Counting in fives will be much faster than counting them all one by one.

The students use the hundreds chart to help them count the cucumbers. They start at 5 and count every fifth number. They stop when they have counted all ten plants.

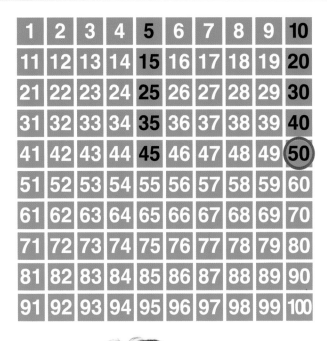

1	2	3	4	5	6	7	8	9	10
11	12	13	14	15	16	17	18	19	20
21	22	23	24	25	26	27	28	29	30
31	32	33	34	35	36	37	38	39	40
41	42	43	44	45	46	47	48	49	50
51	52	53	54	55	56	57	58	59	60
61	62	63	64	65	66	67	68	69	70
71	72	73	74	75	76	77	78	79	80
81	82	83	84	85	86	87	88	89	90
91	92	93	94	95	96	97	98	99	100

There are 50 cucumbers in total.

50 Cucumbers

Skip counting is extra helpful for counting large numbers quickly. There are eight strawberry plants in the garden. Each plant has grown ten strawberries. Maya can skip count the strawberries by tens.

1	2	3	4	5	6	7	8	9	10
11	12	13	14	15	16	17	18	19	20
21	22	23	24	25	26	27	28	29	30
31	32	33	34	35	36	37	38	39	40
41	42	43	44	45	46	47	48	49	50
51	52	53	54	55	56	57	58	59	60
61	62	63	64	65	66	67	68	69	70
	73	74	75	76	77	78	79	80	
		83	84	85	86	87	88	89	90
		93	94	95	96	97	98	99	100

Eight strawberry plants with 10 strawberries each makes 80 strawberries!

Finally, Zoë helps Robert count the blueberries. There are nine blueberry bushes. Each bush has 100 blueberries. The students can skip count the blueberries by hundreds. They start at 100. The second bush makes 200 and the third makes 300.

400... 500... 600... ...700...800...900! That was much faster!

Ali wrote all the numbers on the board and took it to Professor Tangent. Zoë's clever counting tips helped the students count each type of fruit and vegetable quickly.

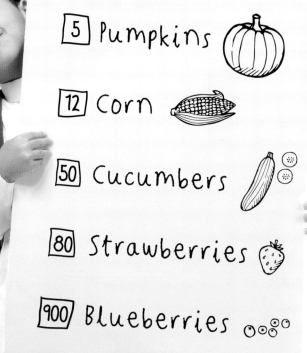

5 Pumpkins

12 Corn

50 Cucumbers

80 Strawberries

900 Blueberries

Thanks to Zoë, the students have plenty of time left over to enjoy some delicious, fresh fruit!

Can you count by threes to see how many potatoes the children grew?

1	2	3	4	5	6	7	8	9	10
11	12	13	14	15	16	17	18	19	20
21	22	23	24	25	26	27	28	29	30
31	32	33	34	35	36	37	38	39	40
41	42	43	44	45	46	47	48	49	50
51	52	53	54	55	56	57	58	59	60
61	62	63	64	65	66	67	68	69	70
71	72	73	74	75	76	77	78	79	80
81	82	83	84	85	86	87	88	89	90
91	92	93	94	95	96	97	98	99	100

Answer: 36

How many seeds do the students have for next year? Each packet has 10 seeds inside.

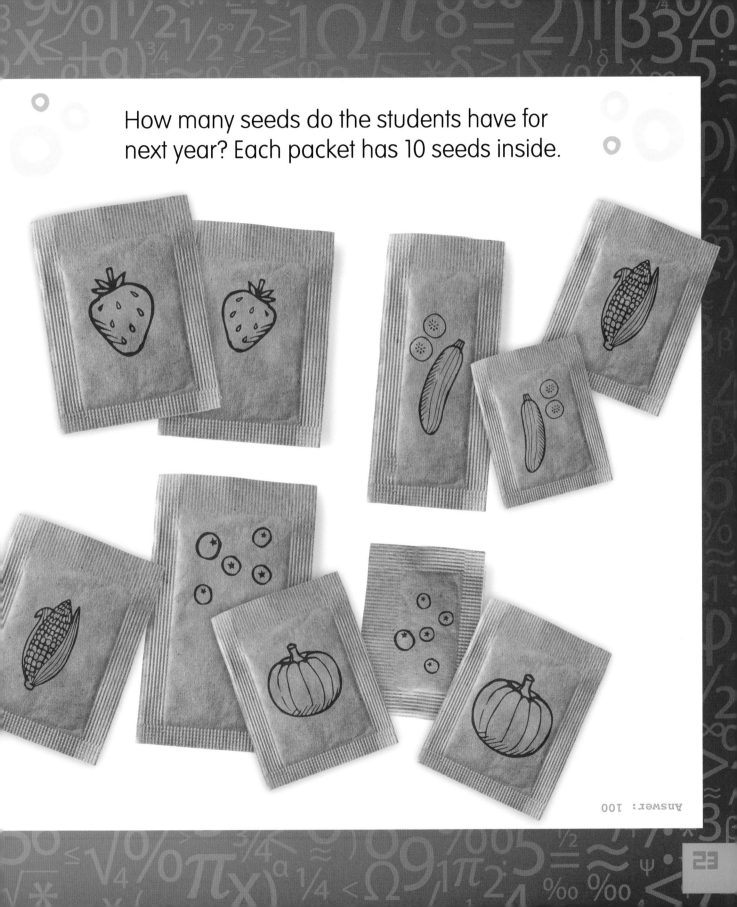

GLOSSARY

COBS — The long, central part of an ear of corn on which kernels grow

COUNTING — Say numbers in order, starting with one

HUNDREDS CHART — A chart with rows of numbers from one to one hundred

SEEDS — Small, hard parts of plants from which new plants grow

SKIP COUNTING — Counting by a number other than one

STALK — The tall, main stem of a plant

TOTAL — A final number reached by adding other numbers together

INDEX